FROM THE AUTHOR OF MONEY MATTERS

MONEY
NUGGETS

QUOTES THAT WILL CHANGE HOW YOU THINK ABOUT MONEY AND INSPIRE YOU TO BUILD WEALTH

MASTER FINANCIAL COACH
KAREN FORD

Copyright © 2018 Karen Ford
MONEY NUGGETS

Printed in the USA

Published by KBF Management Company, Fairmont, WV

Prepared for publication by www.wendykwalters.com

ISBN (print): 978-0-9995415-4-8
ISBN (kindle): 978-0-9995415-5-5

All Rights Reserved. This book is protected by the copyright laws of the United States of America. This book may not be copied or reprinted for commercial gain or profit. The use of short quotations is permitted. Permission will be granted upon request. The author guarantees all contents are original and do not infringe upon the legal rights of any other person or work.

Scripture has been taken from the *Holy Bible, New International Version*, NIV. Copyright © 1973, 1978, 1984 by the International Bible Society. Used by permission of Zondervan Publishing House. All rights reserved.

To Contact the Author: www.karenford.org

MONEY NUGGETS

This book is presented to

_____

by

_____

MONEY NUGGETS

"This book is an inspirational guide that teaches how to manage the money God provides to us through work, inheritance, gifts, and increase."

CANDY CALENTINE
Grandmother of Five

"Steps to common sense money management:

```
                              Trust
                     Control ┌──────
             Invest ┌────────
      Plan ┌────────
    ───────
```

Money Nuggets provides good advice from a respected financial coach."

PAUL WHITE
Retired

Will you manage your money or will it remain?

People who don't manage their money will soon wonder where it went.

A man asked Jesus what he needed to do, saying he had already fulfilled all the law. When Jesus told him to sell all he had and give to the poor, the man became saddened.

God is looking for the heart of love. Anytime He gives us an instruction regarding money, it will reveal a heart issue.

Will you do what He asks?

Money …

You can make it—

maintain it—

manage it!

You can have money as long as money doesn't have you!

Consumer debt strips your future to enhance your present.

—DR. KEITH JOHNSON

Manage your money or you will wonder where it went!

Prevent wondering by managing your money!

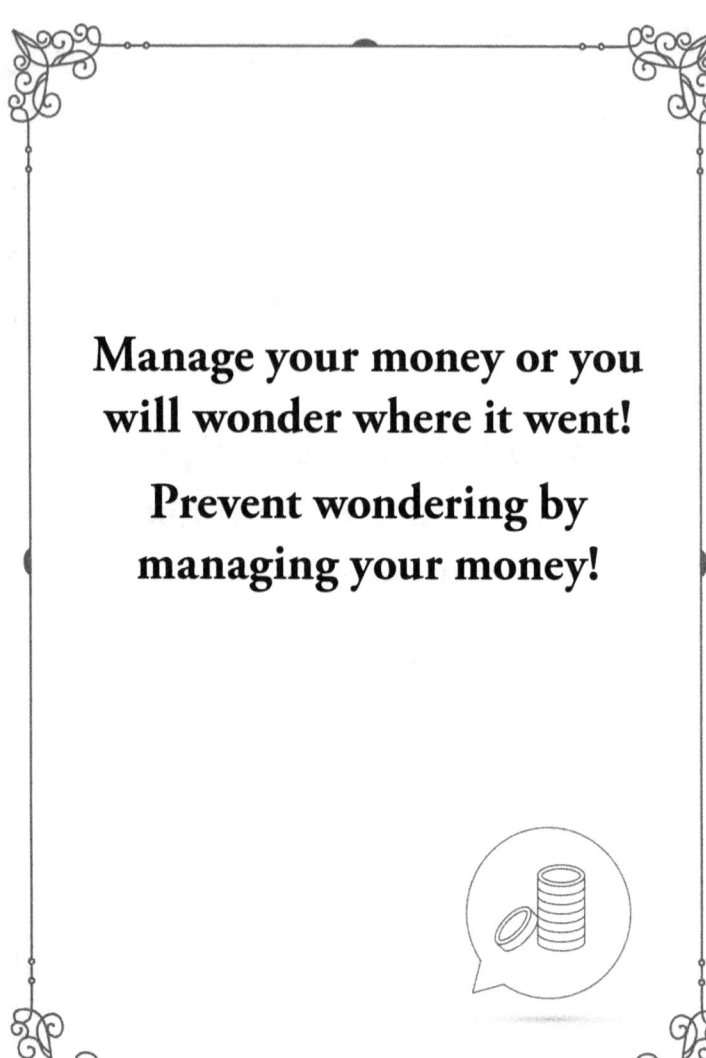

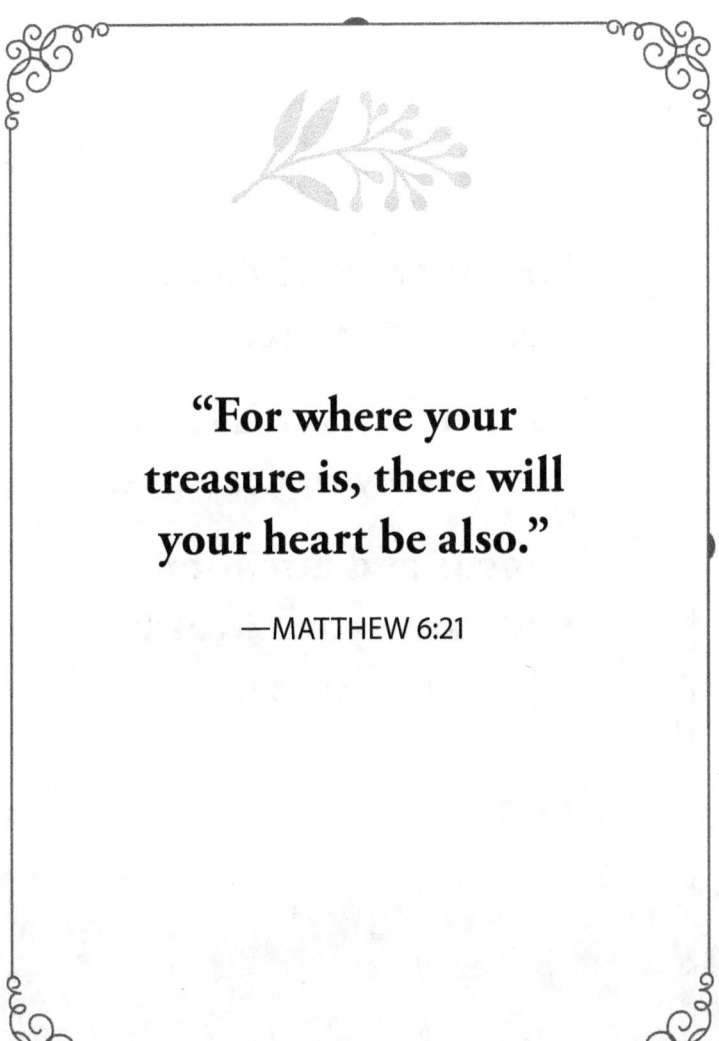

"For where your treasure is, there will your heart be also."

—MATTHEW 6:21

Your money will either decrease or increase!

Lack of focus will cause your money to decrease.

Focus and attention will cause your wealth to increase!

When making a purchase
is it a want or a need?

Is this life-sustaining or
fulfillment of greed?

If you buy all your wants you
will find much concern.

You'll soon beg for your needs
if you spend all you earn.

**Beg, borrow, or budget—
the choice is yours.**

**Control your money
and change your life!**

If you can believe it, you can do it!

See yourself completely debt free and before you know it, debt free you will be!

Dream big.

Think big.

Invest big.

**Borrowing today,
is taking from your future!**

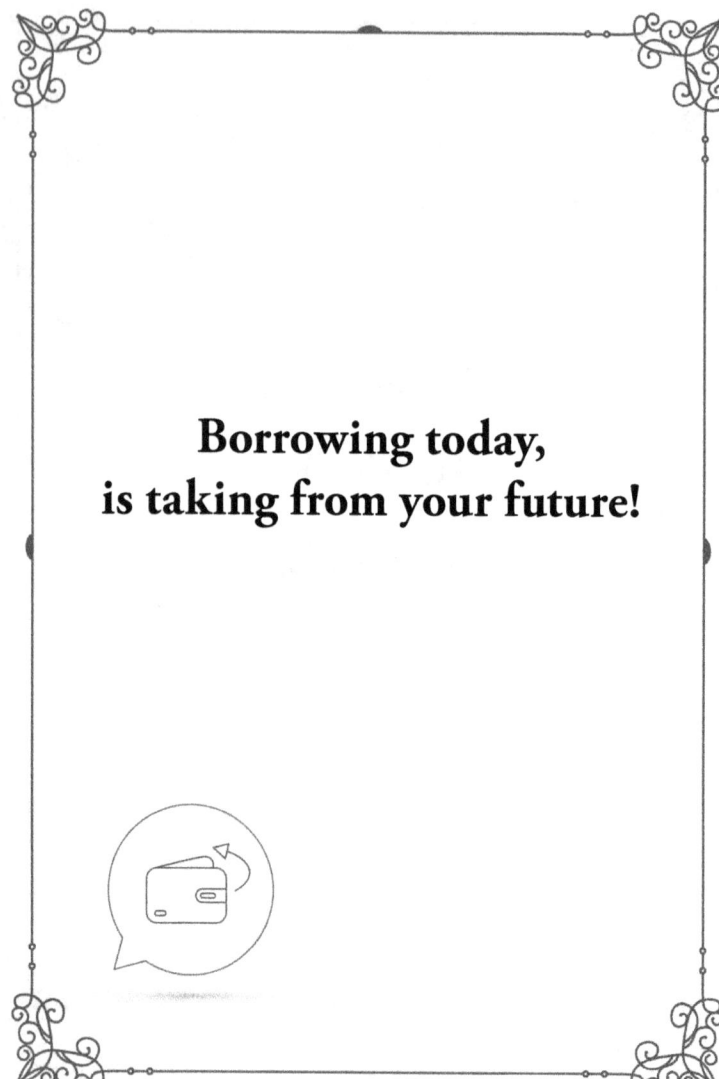

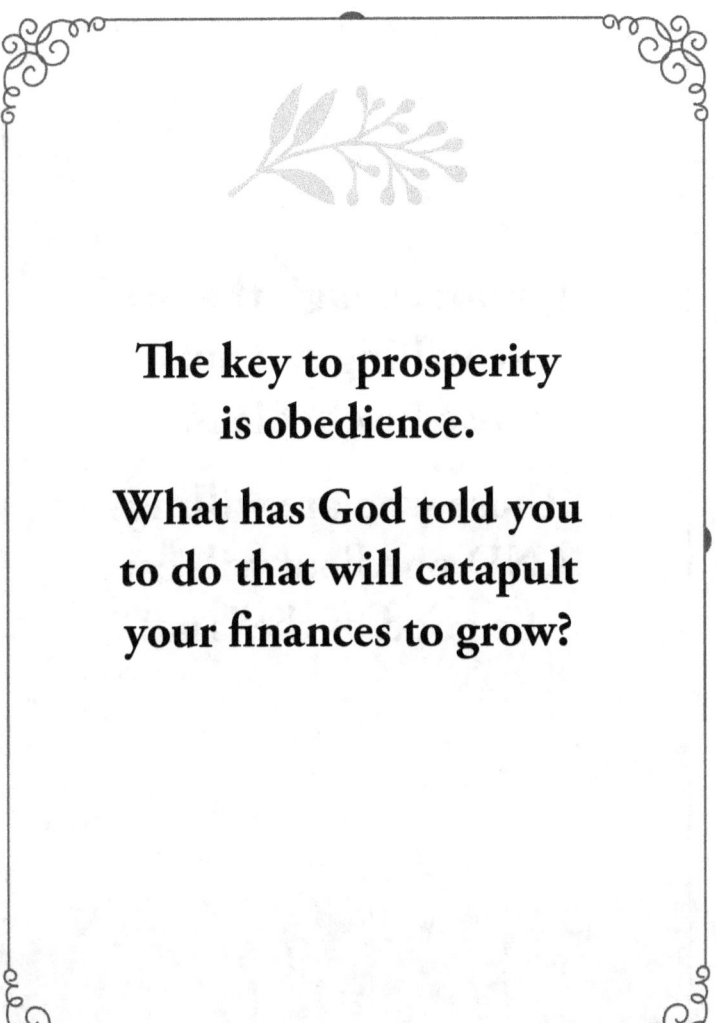

The key to prosperity is obedience.

What has God told you to do that will catapult your finances to grow?

It's not enough that we are willing, we must also be obedient.

Those who are willing AND obedient will eat the good of the land!

MONEY NUGGETS

**If you can see it,
you can achieve it!**

Be faithful!

A faithful man is bound to be blessed!

> **"Dishonest money dwindles away, but whoever gathers money little by little makes it grow."**
>
> —PROVERBS 13:11

Investing prepares you for the future!

The potential of a seed cannot be realized until it is sown.

Mind Over Money:

Becoming wealthy begins with a mindset.

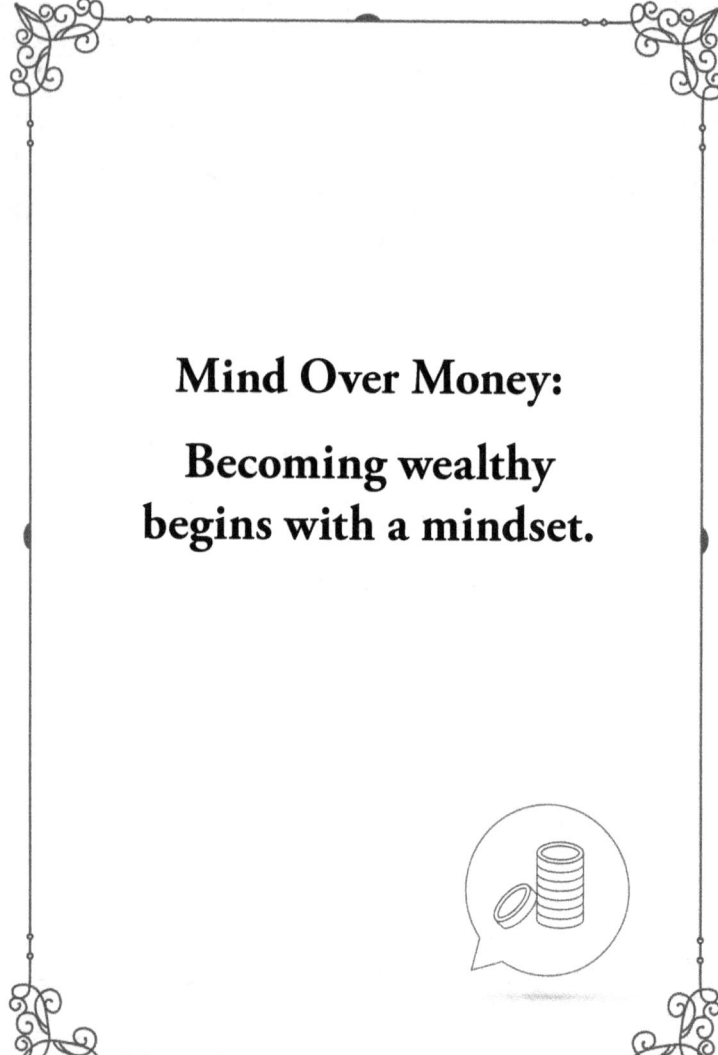

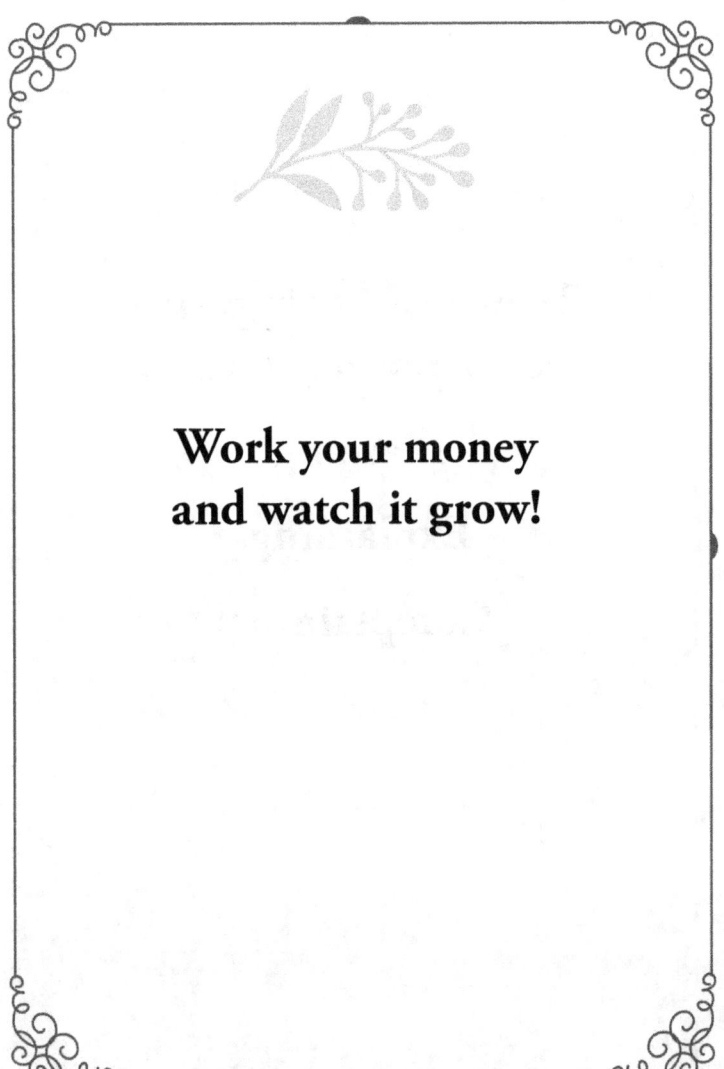

**Work your money
and watch it grow!**

There are 3 things that reveal a poverty mindset:

Blaming,

Explaining,

Complaining!

There are 3 things that reveal a prosperity mindset:

Believing,

Achieving,

Receiving!

Plan your work.

Work your plan.

You'll soon have money from the works of your hand.

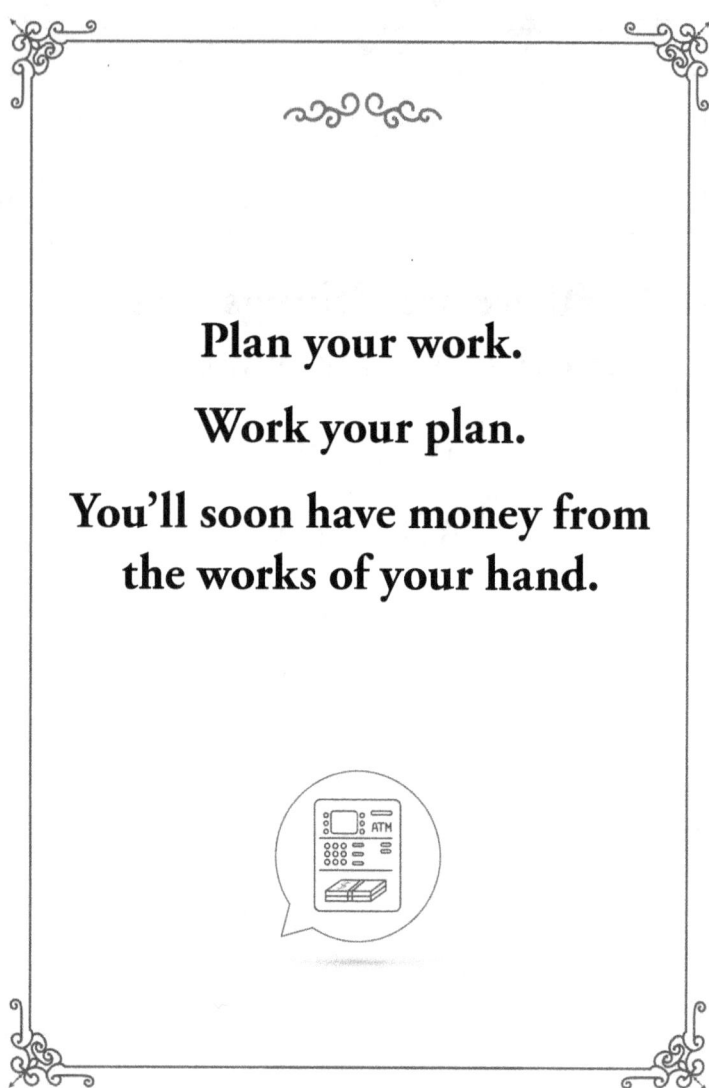

MONEY NUGGETS

> "Lazy hands make for poverty, but diligent hands bring wealth."
>
> —PROVERBS 10:4

If you are faithful with a little money, you will receive more!

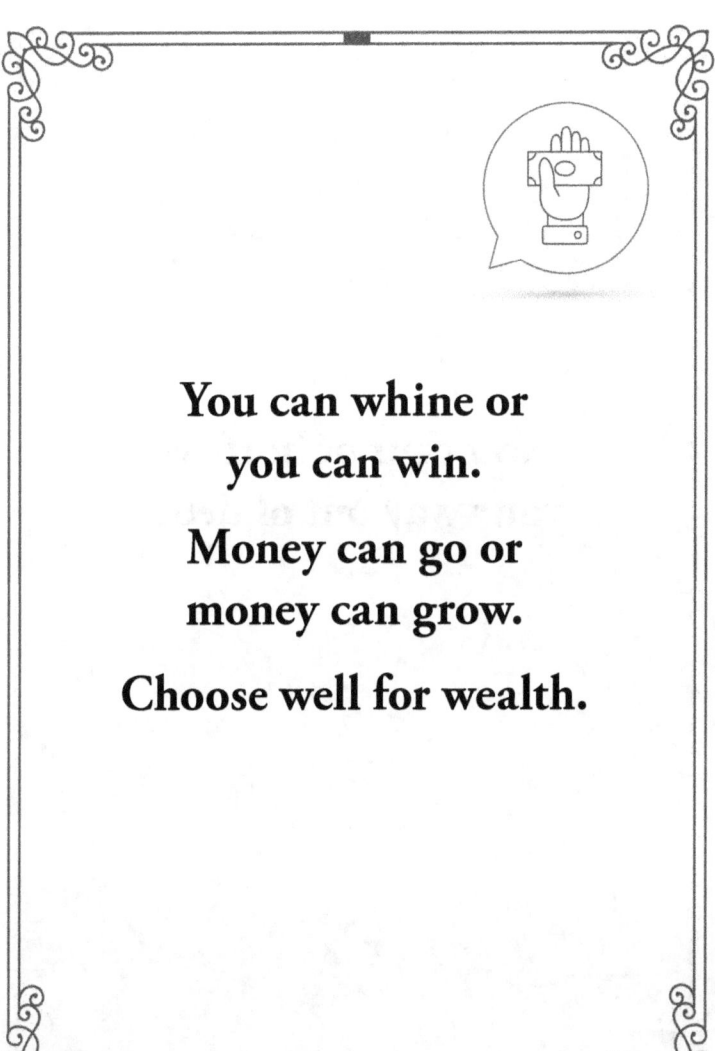

You can whine or you can win.

Money can go or money can grow.

Choose well for wealth.

**You cannot borrow
your way out of debt.**

Control your money or the lack of money will soon control you.

> "Those who trust in themselves are fools, but those who walk in wisdom are kept safe."
>
> —PROVERBS 28:26

Wisdom demands we save for the future.

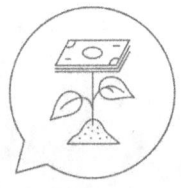

Put God first and everything else will line up.

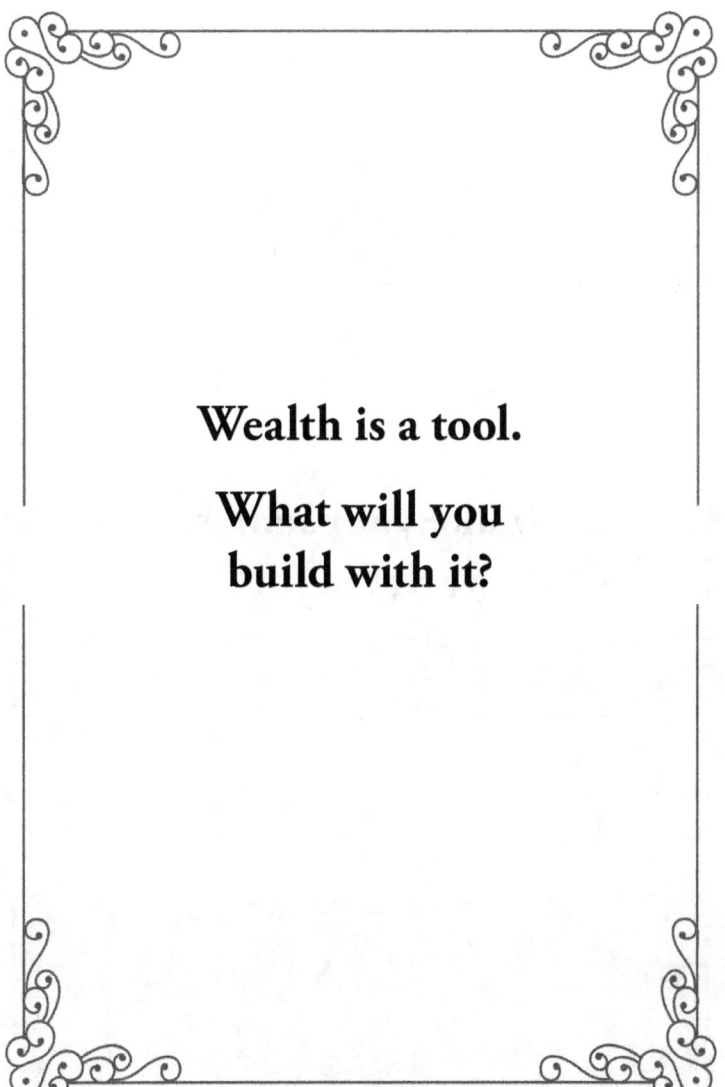

Wealth is a tool.

What will you build with it?

Make your money work for you.

Spending too much makes your money stall.

Debt will cause you to hit a wall.

Investment allows you to bring in a haul!

When dealing with money, planning is key!

Save, invest, and live debt free!

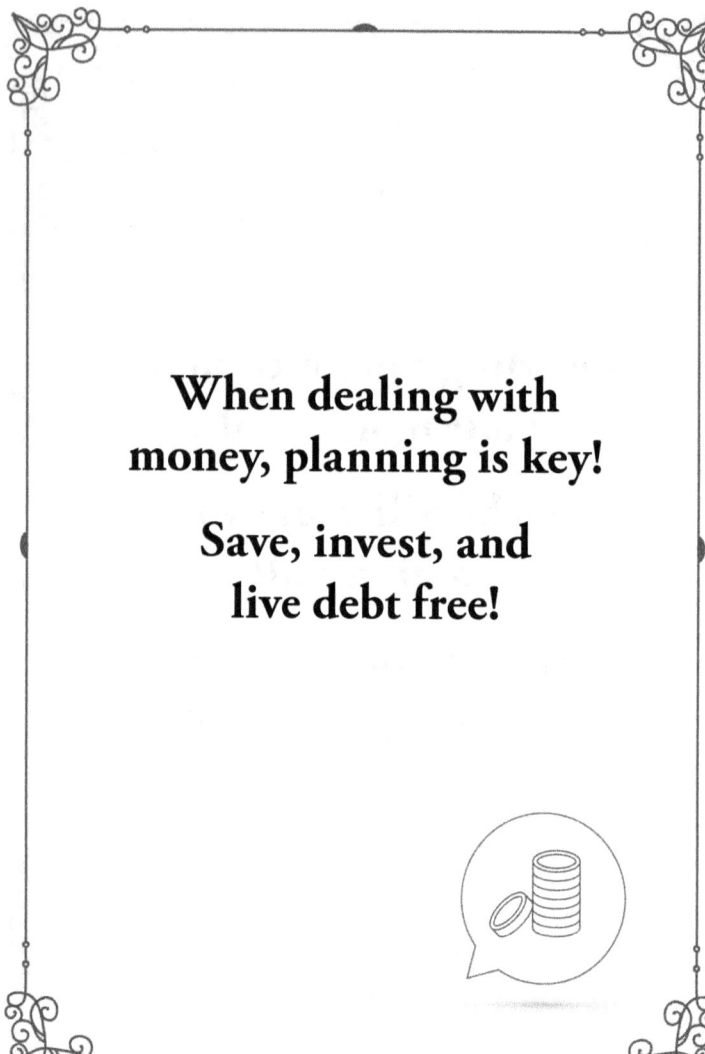

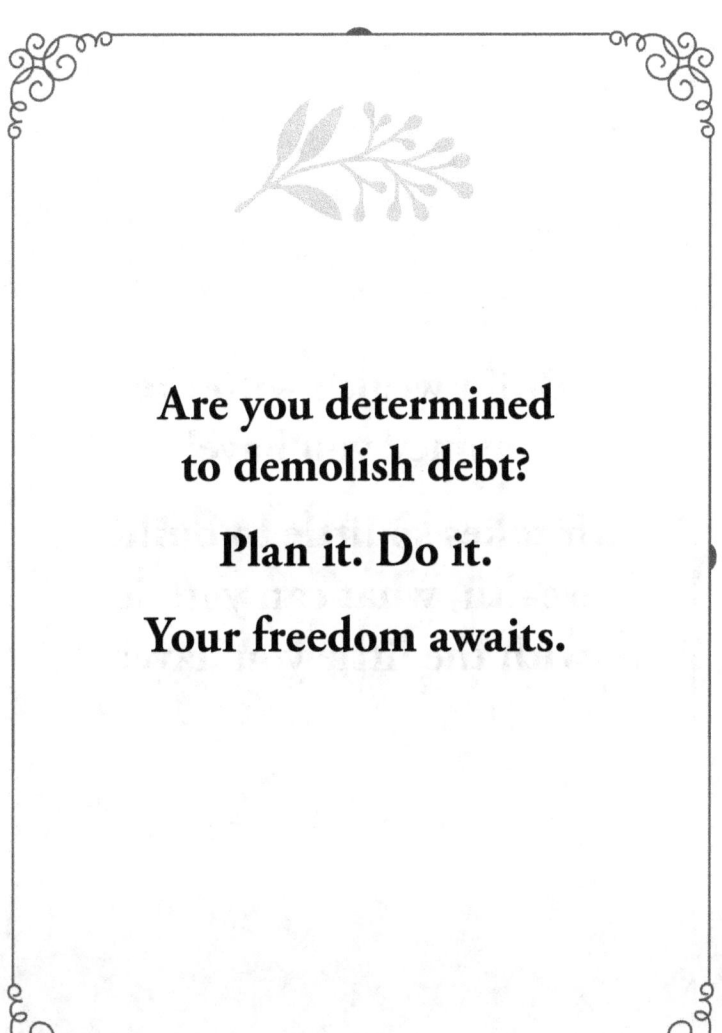

Are you determined to demolish debt?

Plan it. Do it.

Your freedom awaits.

Build wealth with the money you have!

It takes so little to build wealth, what can you do with the little you have?

Remain humble when dealing with money.

If you defend your finances, you won't change them.

People who don't believe for the future spend money in the now!

Prosperity is in direct correlation to obedience.

What direction has God given you?

Walk it out and obey to see abundance in your finances.

Are you diligent?

Are you a hard worker?

Be like the ant!

Prepare,

Position,

Persist!

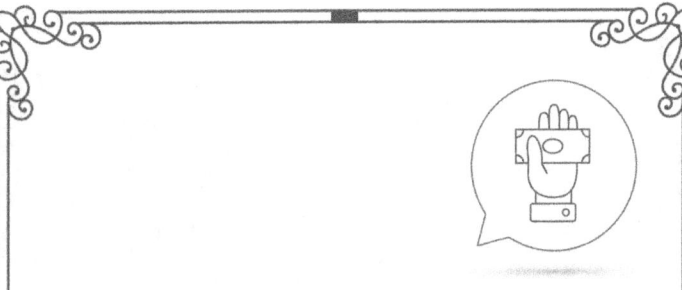

When you buy with cash you will spend less than when using a credit or debit card.

Spending cash is an important key to spending less.

Time is a precious commodity.

Spend it wisely for a rich return.

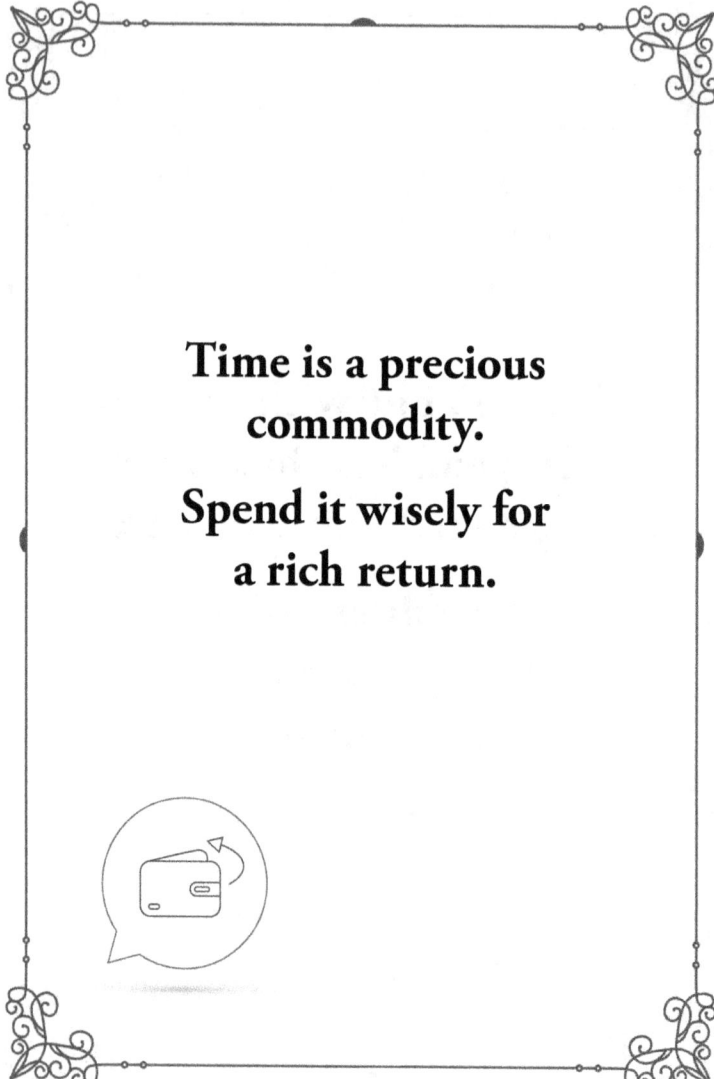

Goals that are never set will never be reached.

What goals will you set today?

How we spend money reveals our character.

What do your spending habits say about you?

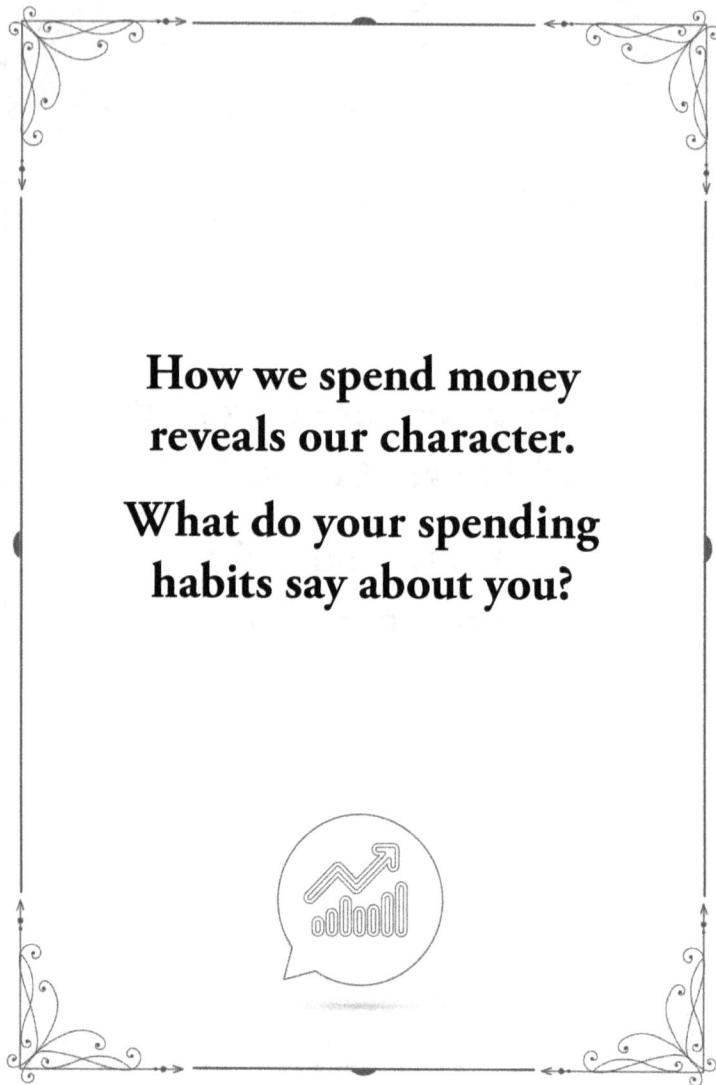

"One person gives freely, yet gains even more; another withholds unduly, but comes to poverty.

A generous person will prosper; whoever refreshes others will be refreshed."

—PROVERBS 11:24-25

**God wants you to
have wealth!**

**He desires all His children to
be wealthy so they have more
than enough to help others.**

**You are blessed to
be a blessing.**

God invests in you, expecting a return on His investment.

Can He trust you?

What return will you bring Him?

If God doesn't want us to have wealth, then why does He give us the power to get wealth?

Don't buy your wants and beg your needs.

This is a sign of immaturity.

Be patient. Save for your wants and don't spend what you don't have.

There is no reward without risk.

What risks are you willing to take today that will catapult your finances tomorrow?

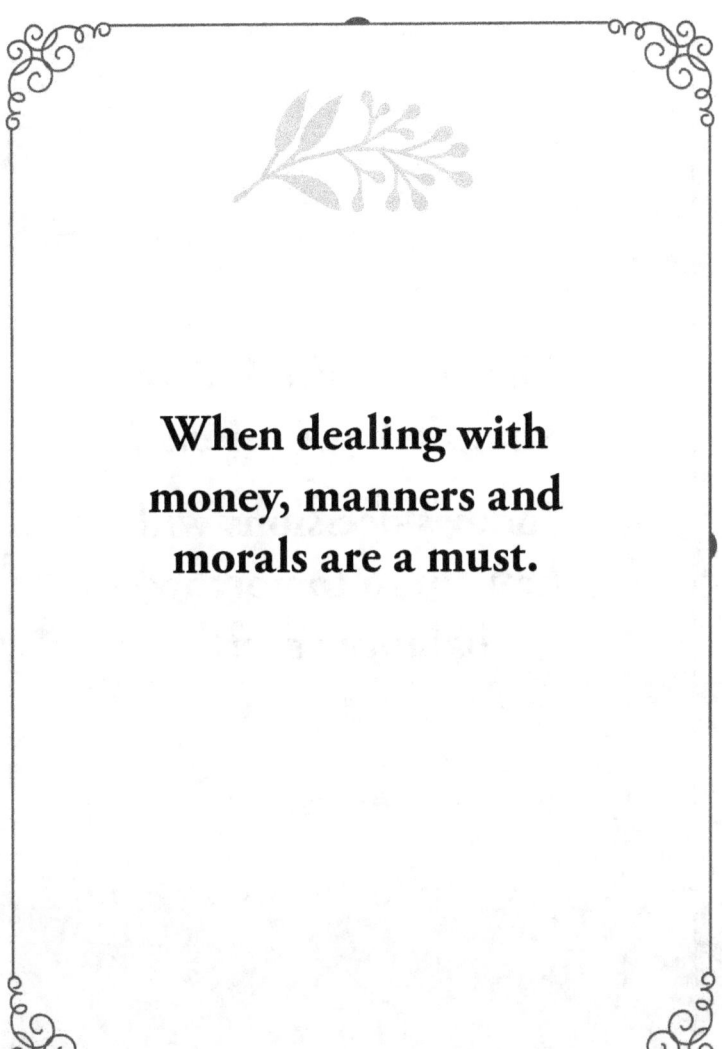

When dealing with money, manners and morals are a must.

Wealth is a product of your daily decisions!

Today's decisions will show up in tomorrow's balance sheet.

When God can trust you, whatever you put your hand to will prosper.

Trust is a key to prosperity!

"The LORD will open the heavens—the storehouse of His bounty—to send rain on your land in season and to bless all the work of your hands. You will lend to many nations but will borrow from none."

—DEUTERONOMY 28:12

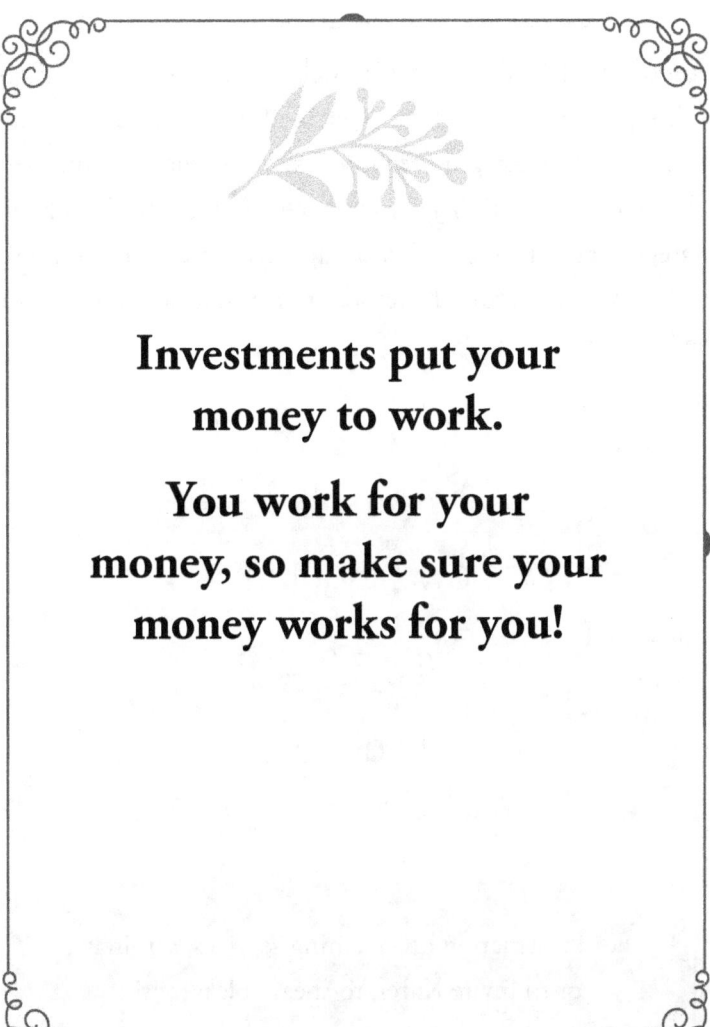

Investments put your money to work.

You work for your money, so make sure your money works for you!

MONEY NUGGETS

KBF MONEY MANAGING

Do you need help eliminating debt, planning cash flow, and building wealth? As a Master Certified Financial Coach, Karen Ford's money managing techniques will guide you into living debt free. She will help you create and execute budgeting strategies and tackle planning for retirement as you build wealth for your future. Karen offers seminars and coaching for the following:

- keys for debt demolition
- cash flow planning
- how to retire well
- how to build wealth

> For information on coaching services, seminars, or to invite Karen to speak, please visit:
>
> **www.karenford.org**

www.ingramcontent.com/pod-product-compliance
Lightning Source LLC
Chambersburg PA
CBHW070440010526
44118CB00014B/2122